AFRICAN MYTHOLOGY

Titles in the Mythology Series:

African Mythology
ISBN 0-7660-2125-4

American Indian Mythology
ISBN 0-7660-1411-8

Chinese Mythology
ISBN 0-7660-1412-6

Egyptian Mythology
ISBN 0-7660-1407-X

*Gods and Goddesses in
Greek Mythology*
ISBN 0-7660-1408-8

*Heroes in
Greek Mythology*
ISBN 0-7660-1560-2

*The Iliad and the Odyssey in
Greek Mythology*
ISBN 0-7660-1561-0

Inuit Mythology
ISBN 0-7660-1559-9

*King Arthur and His Knights
in Mythology*
ISBN 0-7660-1914-4

Mayan and Aztec Mythology
ISBN 0-7660-1409-6

Roman Mythology
ISBN 0-7660-1558-0

~ MYTHOLOGY ~

AFRICAN MYTHOLOGY

Linda Jacobs Altman

Enslow Publishers, Inc.

40 Industrial Road   PO Box 38
Box 398   Aldershot
Berkeley Heights, NJ 07922 Hants GU12 6BP
USA   UK
http://www.enslow.com

For Zachary and Lauren
May you always love stories of far
away and long ago

Copyright © 2003 by Linda Jacobs Altman

Library of Congress Cataloging-in-Publication Data

Altman, Linda Jacobs, 1943–
    African mythology / Linda Jacobs Altman.
        p. cm. — (Mythology)
    Summary: A collection of myths shaped by the cultures and beliefs of
Africa, featuring creator gods, tricksters, shape-changing animals, and heroes
who overcome unthinkable hardship.
    Includes bibliographical references (p.) and index.
    ISBN 0-7660-2125-4
    1. Mythology, African. [1. Mythology, African.] I. Title. II. Series: Mythology
(Berkeley Heights, N.J.)
    BL2400.A48 2003
    299'.62—dc21   2002153079

Printed in the United States of America

10 9 8 7 6 5 4 3 2 1

Cover and Illustrations by William Sauts Bock

 CONTENTS

 PREFACE

Africa is a place of extremes, from bone-dry deserts to steamy jungles and broad, grassland plains. It was on this continent of contrasts that humankind was born. Here, the ancestors of humanity first walked on two legs instead of four. Here, they began to speak, learned to make tools, and became *Homo sapiens*, the animal that thinks.

There is no "African nation" in the sense that there is, for example, an "American nation" or a "Japanese nation." Africa has some fifty different nations within its nearly 12 million square miles (31 million square kilometers) of territory. Those nations in turn are populated by some three thousand groups, speaking at least a thousand different languages.

This does not mean that African groups have nothing in common with one another. It does mean that statements about Africa as a whole will not be true of all people in all circumstances. It also means that the term "African" covers a rich variety of cultural and mythological traditions.

The Lay of the Land

African geography is as varied as African culture. The continent is a vast plateau, or raised flatland. It is divided almost in half by the equator, an imaginary line circling the center of Earth.

There are many regions and subregions on the continent, but the most basic categories are deserts, jungles, and grassland plains, or savannas. Africa is bordered by the Mediterranean Sea on the north, the Atlantic Ocean on the west, and the Indian Ocean on the east.

The Sahara desert in the northwest is the largest desert

in the world. In this place of shifting sands and little water, temperatures can reach 130°F (54.4°C) on a summer afternoon. In the south, the barren sands of the Sahara give way to a semi-arid region known as the Sahel. It ranges from 125 to 250 miles (200 to 400 kilometers) wide and gradually merges into the jungle, or tropical forest.[1]

This is equatorial Africa—a place of lush vegetation, of strange creatures and hidden dangers. The trees form a canopy that shelters the forest floor from direct sunlight. Tangles of vines, mosses, and fungi make the deep jungle impassable. Humans and animals alike must travel on well-worn trails or clear the underbrush as they move.

Beyond the jungle lies the southern savanna, a grassland plain that is home to animals that most non-Africans only see in the zoo. Here are oddities like the giraffe and the rhinoceros, along with beautiful but deadly hunters like the lion and the cheetah.

At its southern boundaries, the savanna meets an unusual region known as the Kalahari Desert. The Kalahari looks more like a grassland than a desert, but it has almost no surface water. A brief rainy season fills up water holes for a time, but they soon go dry. Animals come when the watering holes are full and leave when the water is gone.

The People and the Cultures

Africans have traditionally lived in tribal communities. A tribe is a group of people sharing common ancestry, customs, language, and beliefs.

These groups may be large or small. Some are led by powerful chiefs and some are more egalitarian (based on social equality). Some have formal laws and some do not. All have standards of social behavior, but what is acceptable in one culture may be downright criminal in another. Given all these differences and many more besides, it is difficult to classify these groups culturally. Some scholars fall back on an old standby: geography. Cultures that share an environment tend to share other traits, as well.

Geography makes at least one division easy: North African tribes as a group are very different from those of sub-Saharan Africa, or "black Africa," as it is sometimes called. Most North African peoples are Arabs and Berbers who practice the Muslim religion and speak Arabic as their main language.

In ancient times, many of them were traders. Their camel caravans transported goods along the trans-Sahara trade routes. Others were nomadic herders, traveling from one source of water to another with the goats they raised for milk and meat.

In sub-Saharan Africa, cultural and religious traditions are amazingly varied. There are Arabic-speaking Muslims along the Saharan border and on the coasts. In the south, Christianity and European languages are prominent. Throughout the region, many people remain faithful to traditional African ways of life.

In African tradition, tribal identity is still important. Many sub-Saharan Africans live in small tribal villages, keeping their distance from outsiders. Though they may have a few modern conveniences, the old traditions still shape their lives. For example, many people still live in extended families: several generations together under the leadership of the eldest male.

History and Prehistory

Traditional Africans share an interesting view of time and history. They do not keep time by the clock or the calendar, but by events. Philosopher John S. Mbiti gave

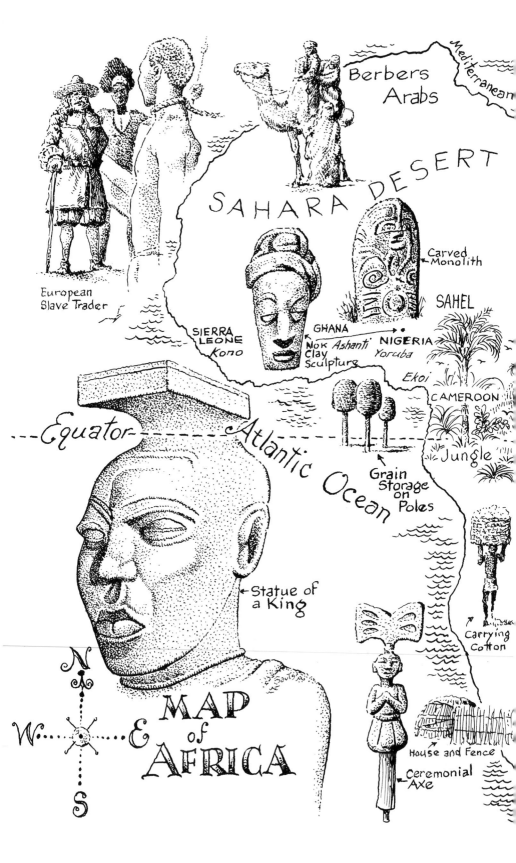

Berbers
Arabs

Mediterranean

SAHARA DESERT

European
Slave Trader

SIERRA
LEONE
Kono

Carved
Monolith

SAHEL

GHANA

Nok *Ashanti*
Clay
Sculpture

NIGERIA
Yoruba

Ekoi

CAMEROON

Jungle

Equator

Atlantic Ocean

Grain
Storage
on
Poles

Statue of
a King

Carrying
Cotton

N
W   E
S

MAP
of
AFRICA

House and Fence

Ceremonial
Axe

Sea

carvings of Swords on Rock

MUSLIM MEN

Village

Mother and Child Gather Food →

← Maise

Carvings on Adobe Building

Agriculture
KENYA

Equator

Tropical Forests

Chaga
wheat
TANZANIA

Rhinoceros

Cheetah   Giraffe

SAVANNAS

Mud Granary for Storing Grain

Indian Ocean

Kung

Iron Spear Point

Clay Vessel

Lion and Hunter

KALAHARI DESERT

Hunter With Bow →

a dramatic example of this in his book *African Religions and Philosophy*:

> the rising of the sun is an event which is recognized by the whole community. It does not matter . . . whether the sun rises at 5 A.M. or 7 A.M., so long as it rises. When a person says that he will meet another at sunrise, it does not matter whether the meeting takes place at 5 A.M. or 7 A.M., so long as it is during the general period of sunrise.[2]

In the place where humankind was born, it seems fitting that time should be tied to the endless rhythms of nature. It was on the African savanna nearly 4 million years ago that the earliest human ancestor first appeared.[3] *Australopithecus* could not talk or reason. What it could do was walk upright on two legs instead of four. This freed the hands for making and using tools—and began the long process of human development.

Physically modern humans first appeared in Africa around 100,000 years ago. They used stone tools such as hand axes and scrapers. Later, they learned to shape stones into sharp-pointed spearheads and then to make bows and arrows. With these weapons, hunters could pursue bigger, faster animals.

Thus the hunter-gatherer culture was born. People lived and traveled together, often in extended family groups. The men hunted game while the women and children gathered nuts, seeds, and edible plants.

This began to change with the Agricultural Revolution, some ten to twelve thousand years ago. Farmers settled in one place to plant and tend their crops. They built homes and villages. Later, they built cities and even empires. Because of these new social institutions, technology began to develop at a faster pace.

About 2,500 years ago, the Stone Age began giving way to the Iron Age. The Nok people, who lived in what is now Nigeria, were among the first develop iron smelting (melting iron ore so it can be formed into tools and weapons).

Archeologists, scientists who study ancient cultures, have found beautiful *terra cotta* (baked clay) sculptures at Nok sites. Evidence suggests a well-organized and prosperous society that spread its culture through the region.

Lost Empires

The Nok culture may well have influenced later kingdoms and empires. A kingdom is a nation-state ruled by a monarch (king or queen). It generally has well-defined boundaries and a strong sense of national identity. An empire may rule over a number of nation-states that are otherwise not connected to one another.

One of the earliest African empires, the Empire of Ghana, was founded in the early tenth century. There is no connection between ancient Ghana and the modern nation which shares its name. The two are separated by 400 miles (644 kilometers) and nine centuries.

Ancient Ghana was known for its gold. Vast quantities came from its mines and were transported by camel caravans into the kingdoms of the Sahara. Along the trade routes of ancient Africa, legends of Ghana's wealth traveled with the caravans.

Ghana's power began to decline with the discovery of new gold deposits in other parts of Africa. During the same period, a long drought almost destroyed Ghana's agriculture. By the middle of the twelfth century, what remained of Ghana was absorbed into the new Empire of Mali.

Another mysterious civilization had its beginnings on a plateau in Zimbabwe at the beginning of the thirteenth century. Even today, the ruin of a great stone fortress still glowers down on the surrounding grassland. For three hundred years, this was the seat of power of an empire known as Great Zimbabwe.

The identity of the builders is uncertain, but their skill is not. The fortress could withstand even the fiercest attack. For additional protection, it could only be approached through a series of passes, or corridors, so narrow that visitors could only enter single-file. No would-be invader could get an army through the passes quickly enough to mount an assault.

It appears that the builders did their job well. There are no signs that Great Zimbabwe was ever conquered by an enemy. In the early fifteenth century, it was simply abandoned. The exact reason is unknown, but evidence suggests that overfarming of the surrounding countryside was the culprit. The soil became depleted and could not produce enough food for the royal court.[4]

The Slave Trade

The trappings of empire were not limited to stone fortresses. Kings and other powerful men also owned slaves. They were mostly used as household servants and as living proof of the wealth and importance of their masters.

Although all slavery is objectionable today, African forms were mild until the international trade began. Early slavery in Africa was not a profit-making business, nor was slave labor necessary for economic survival.

Slavery-for-profit began when Portuguese traders arrived on the northwestern coast of Africa in 1444. For over seventy years, the traders took their human cargo to European ports. Not until 1518 did they begin transporting slaves directly from Africa to the Americas. Over time, the Spanish, the Dutch, the British, and the French got involved in this transatlantic trade.

To meet the growing demand, African slave raiders made regular trips into the interior, capturing tens of thousands of people. They brought these captives back to the coast and sold them to European dealers. Most of these slaves were sent to the Americas.

The Middle Passage, as the route was called, was a brutal journey. People were packed together in the bowels of the ship. There was no light or fresh air and only enough food and water to keep them barely alive. Many died from starvation, disease, or exposure. Their bodies were thrown overboard like so much garbage.

Conditions on the Passage were so terrible that even some slave owners claimed to be shocked. The more people learned about the "business" of slave trading, the more they realized that it had to end. In the early nineteenth century, one slaving nation after another outlawed the Atlantic trade.

It had lasted for over three hundred years. In that time, at least 10 million Africans were kidnapped and sold into slavery.[5] Whole villages were destroyed and families were torn apart.

Sadly, the African kings who had grown rich dealing in human lives protested the end of the trade. One of the kings of Dahomey (modern Benin) called the slave trade "the ruling principle of my people. It is the source and glory of their wealth."[6]

Colonial Rule

The end of the slave trade did not mean the end of European interest in Africa. In the late nineteenth century, Great Britain, France, Holland, and other countries established colonies there. These colonists did not come as settlers, but as conquerors.

The Europeans had advanced weaponry and a firm

belief in their own superiority. They took control of large areas and administered them for their own benefit.

These colonial powers imposed European standards on African societies. Africans began to adopt Western ways, especially in the cities. Many lost their sense of connection to the old traditions.

They did not lose their interest in freedom, however. In the mid-twentieth century, one African nation after another broke away from colonial rule. These new nations were plagued by poverty. They faced wars, famines, and epidemics of deadly disease.

In the midst of these horrors, Africans began to rediscover their own cultures. They found a history of pain and loss, but also of courage and endurance. They found long-neglected tribal identities and ancient rituals that spoke to the heart. And they found stories: myths and legends that were at once ancient and timeless.

The Stories of Africa

Myths are the stories of a people. They deal with gods and heroes and the origin of things. The themes, or topics, are universal; they appear all over the world. The stories based upon those themes reflect the cultures that produced them.

Because there is no single African culture, there is no single African mythology. Instead, there are many African mythologies—thousands of stories that have been handed down from one generation to another.

The stories in this book show how different African cultures have approached basic mythological themes, such as the creation of the world and the origin of death. Here are creator gods and tricksters, shape-changing animals and heroes who overcome unthinkable hardship. They are the stories of the world, shaped by the cultures and beliefs of Africa.

1

COMING DOWN FROM THE SKY

THE YORUBA OF NIGERIA

This story is a creation myth from the Yoruban people of Nigeria. The Yoruba are not a single tribe, but a group of tribes that share a mythological tradition and a language. At the beginning of the twenty-first century, about 20 million people spoke some form of this language.[1]

Long before Europeans arrived in Africa, many Yorubas lived in densely populated city-states. Of these, the city of Ife was most important. It was a center of sacred wisdom, and was said to have been founded on the very spot where the god Obatala first came down from the sky.

Obatala formed the world and shaped human beings out of clay, but the Yoruban creation myth does not begin with him. It begins with the mysterious, formless Orisa-nla and a rebellious slave called Atunda. Atunda killed Orisa-nla by rolling a huge boulder down upon him. It smashed Orisa-nla into pieces, and the fragments became the *orishas* (gods).

The *orishas* came into being through the death of an earlier deity, or god. This is fairly common in creation stories; a younger race of gods emerges from an older and more primitive one. It is this younger group that brings order to the world and creates human beings to live there.

For example, in Greek mythology the gods of Olympus were the children of an earlier group of gods called Titans. A terrible war left the Titans defeated and the Olympians triumphant. The god Prometheus then formed human beings out of clay, much as Obatala did in the Yoruban myth.

Obatala is an interesting figure. He is known as "the king of the white cloth," because white is a symbol of creativity and male fertility. He is not all-powerful or all-knowing, nor is he the chief god in the Yoruban pantheon, or group of gods.

The sky god, Olorun, rules the *orishas*. Olorun himself is not all-powerful, but he can do things that the other *orishas* cannot. When Obatala wants light in his new-made world, he must call upon Olorun to make the sun. Obatala can form people out of clay, but only Olorun can give them the breath of life.

When Obatala decides to make a world, he has no idea where to start. He goes to the seer, Orunmila, who can probe the mysteries of life. Orunmila tells Obatala what needs to be done.

Obatala faces many problems, but he does not give up. When the world he makes turns out to be imperfect, he does not stop loving it. He even admits his own mistakes and tries to repair the damage.

Obatala's imperfections made him one of the most loved gods in the Yoruban pantheon. His appeal has proved to be timeless. Even today, traditional Yorubas honor Obatala and seek to live by the standards he taught them.

COMING DOWN
FROM THE SKY

Long ago, before Earth was made, there was only sky above and sea below. The sea was gray and silent, a place of mists and wild marshes. Nothing lived; no creature of land or sea or sky. No people.

The *orisha* Obatala looked down from the sky and did not like what he saw. There was nothing down there to delight the eye or capture the heart. The sea should have land and the land should have life.

Perhaps he should make a world.

After thinking on this for a time, Obatala went to tell the sky god, Olorun, about his idea.

"Yes," said Olorun, "things would be more interesting with some life down there. But it would be a long and difficult task. How would you do it?"

Obatala did not answer because he had no idea how to go about building a world. So he went to see Orunmila, the diviner, who could peer into the secrets of existence.

"I want to build a world on the sea below," he said. "Tell me where to start."

Orunmila took sixteen palm nuts into his hand and scattered them over a tray. He studied the pattern they made for a time, and then he gathered up the palm nuts and threw them again. This he did many times—casting and reading, then casting again and reading again. At last, he gathered up the palm nuts and put them away.

"This is how you start," he said. "Climb down to the sea on a golden chain that is hooked onto the edge of the sky. Take four things with you: a white hen, a black cat, a snail shell full of sand, and a palm nut."

Obatala could not help wondering how a hen, a cat, a shell, and a palm nut could help him build a world. Still, he trusted the wisdom of Orunmila. Obatala went to the goldsmith and asked him to make a chain long enough to reach down to the sea.

The goldsmith looked at his supply of gold and shook his head. "This is barely enough to start. Where will you ever find so much gold?"

"I'll find it," said Obatala. "Start working."

So the goldsmith started working and Obatala started looking for gold. He went to all the *orishas*, even Olorun himself. They gave him gold. Some gave all they had, for they realized that a living world in the realm of the sea might be a very good thing to have.

The goldsmith worked and Obatala gathered gold, and the chain grew. When there was no more gold to be had in all the sky, the chain still needed a hook.

"Melt down some of the links to make it," said Obatala.

The goldsmith protested that the chain would be too short to reach the sea.

"Perhaps," said Obatala. "But make it anyway."

The goldsmith made the hook. Olorun himself brought the white hen, the black cat, the snail shell full of sand, and the palm nut. At last Obatala was ready.

He made the hook fast on the edge of the sky and swung himself onto the golden chain. Down he climbed and down, moving away from the light in the sky and into the gray darkness below. The hen clucked, the cat yowled, and Obatala clung to the chain with all his strength.

At last he came to the end. He looked up and could not

see the sky. He looked down and could not see the waters. He hung there between the world below and the world above, wondering what to do.

"The sand," said a voice. It was Orunmila the diviner, guiding him from the sky.

Obatala took the snail shell from the pouch he carried at his waist and poured out the sand.

"The hen," said Orunmila.

Obatala dropped the hen onto the sand. Immediately she began scratching, clucking happily as she scattered sand in every direction. Wherever the sand fell, dry land appeared.

Obatala let go of the chain and dropped to the ground that he had made. He named that place Ife, and there he built a house. There he planted his palm nut, and a palm tree grew. There he lived in a dim and silent world, with only the black cat for company.

"This place is gloomy," he said one day to the cat. "What we need is some light." The cat looked at him with its round, golden eyes and began to purr.

Making light was beyond Obatala's powers, so he waited. In time, Olorun sent his messenger to check on Obatala's progress. Obatala told him what was needed, and the messenger returned to the sky.

Olorun soon made the sun to shine down on Obatala's world.

Obatala loved the light; it reminded him of the sky. The cat took to stretching out in the sunlight for an afternoon's nap.

And so it went. Obatala lived contentedly enough until he realized that the world was still not complete. It needed people.

Obatala began to form them out of clay. The work was hard and the sun was hot, so he grew thirsty. He began to

drink palm wine; a little at first and then more and more. By the time he finished making his people, he could not stand up straight.

When his head began to clear, he called for Olorun. Only the sky god himself could breathe life into the figures that Obatala had made.

Olorun gladly made the people live. They became flesh and bone and started building houses for themselves. This was the beginning of the city of Ife, which grew up in the place that Obatala had first called by that name.

As the people went about their business, Obatala began to notice that he had made mistakes. He had made people with disabilities of many kinds—some with hunchbacks or deformed limbs, some who could not see, and some who could not hear.

Seeing these things, Obatala realized what had happened. These were the people he had formed when he was drunk on palm wine. It had made his fingers clumsy so he could not shape the figures correctly and clouded his mind so he would not notice his mistakes.

Obatala was overcome with sorrow at the pain that he had caused. Then and there, he vowed that he would never again drink palm wine and that he would take all people with disabilities under his protection. And so it was.

Since Obatala made that vow in the long-ago time, his worshipers have refused to drink palm wine. Those who cannot walk or hear or see have called upon him in time of need, knowing that their prayers will always be heard.

QUESTIONS AND ANSWERS

Q: *Why did Obatala dislike looking down at the sea?*

A: Because it was a dark, dead place. Obatala thought it would be more interesting if it were filled with life.

Q: *What question did the sky god Olorun ask that Obatala could not answer?*

A: He asked how Obatala would go about building a world. Obatala had not given any thought to such practical matters. But he did know where to find out. He went to see Orunmila the diviner.

Q: *How did Orunmila find the answer to Olorun's question?*

A: He used a system of divining, or probing, secrets and foretelling the future. This involved casting palm nuts on a special tray and studying the patterns they made when they fell.

Q: *Why did Obatala collect all the gold in the sky?*

A: To make a golden chain long enough to reach from the sky to the sea. Orunmila had told him that he must climb down to the sea on a chain made of gold.

Q: *What did Olorun do when Obatala sent word that the new world needed light?*

A: He made the sun and put it in the sky. The sun gave not only light, but warmth as well. Obatala's world began to flourish.

Q: *When Obatala decided to make people, what was the one thing he could not do for them?*

A: Give them life. Obatala could form the bodies from clay, but only the sky god could make them live. When

Obatala asked Olorun to bring his figures to life, Olorun breathed on them and it was done.

Q: *What was Obatala's great mistake? How did he try to make amends?*

A: He formed some of the people improperly because he was drunk on palm wine. When he saw what he had done, he vowed never to drink palm wine again. He became the protector of all people with disabilities.

Q: *How many actions or events showed that Obatala's power was limited?*

A: There were four: He did not know how to go about building a world; he could not make the sun; he could not bring the people he formed to life; and he made a tragic mistake that harmed humankind.

EXPERT COMMENTARY

The Yoruban creation story grows out of the character and behavior of the *orishas*. These gods are not all-knowing or all-powerful. They are not perfect, but have faults and failings just as humans do.

For example, neither Obatala nor Orunmila know how to make a world. Orunmila learns what is needed by using the same method of divination that humans use to learn the will of the *orishas*. The *Africana Encyclopedia* explains the process:

> The divination system most frequently used is the 16-cowrie shell system [palm nuts are also commonly used] . . . . Typically the diviner throws the cowrie shells onto a special tray. Each orisha corresponds to a specific number and sign, which is indicated by the way the cowrie shells fall. In this manner the diviner [learns] the problem or situation facing the [person], what is causing the problem, and which orisha will help.[2]

Although Obatala made mistakes when he created human beings, the Yoruba do not condemn him. They do not expect their gods to be perfect, and they do not classify them as "bad" or "good." Like humanity itself, the *orishas* are a mixture of both. This is faithfully reflected in Yoruban mythology, as folklorist Harold Courlander explains:

> There is nowhere in the Yoruba oral literature any apparent effort to play down the [bad] side of an orisha's character. The orisha does not have to be "good" to be worshiped . . . . [orishas can] be stern, sometimes even [stubborn], ridiculous or erratic . . . . Like storms, winds and floods, the orishas are forces that exist and have to be coped with.[3]

Imperfect gods made an imperfect world. The Yorubas accept this imperfection as a fact of life. As ethnologist

Sandra Barnes explains, this is very different from most Western views:

> In the West, positive and negative—[also called] evil and good—can be divided into opposing parts [such as] Satan and God. In West Africa, positive and negative power is not separate. Power is singular [one], and therefore what we in the West see as dual and capable of being divided . . . cannot be divided in African thought.[4]

2

THE FIRST PEOPLE AND THE FLOOD

THE EKOI OF NIGERIA AND CAMEROON

Flood myths are as common as creation myths. Accounts of a world-destroying deluge, or flood, appear in the mythologies of most cultures. The same themes appear again and again across widely different cultures.

There are several different patterns of flood myths. In some traditions, a Great Flood appears automatically at the end of every age. No humans cause it by wrongdoing, no god sends it as punishment. It is simply a natural event. This view appears in the mythology of India, where an "age" is billions of years long.

In the West, the most common pattern begins with the gods becoming angry at the misdeeds of humankind. As punishment, they send a great flood. A few righteous people are saved, often by building a boat to ride out the storm. When the flood ends, these people go forth to build a new and better world.

In most African myths, the flood is not a punishment sent to destroy the whole human race. It is more likely to be caused by accident, mistake, or individual wrongdoing.

For example, in one tale the spirit of lightning comes to live on Earth in human form. His very presence unleashes torrential rains, killing many innocent people. A group of hunters track Lightning down and shoot him with poison arrows. When he dies, the rain stops—just in time to avoid the destruction of everything that lives.

In another story, Sun and Moon invite their friend Flood into their home. Flood tries to tell them that their house is too small to contain him, but they insist. When he enters, the waters fill up the entire house. Sun and Moon escape to the roof and leave to make a new home in the sky.

The flood is not started purposely in these stories, nor does it destroy all life on Earth. But it does change that life. Because of the flood, the sun and moon go to the sky where they belong. Because of lightning, many have died, and the world is not the same.

In the Ekoi myth of the first people and the flood, the foolish actions of one man start the deluge. The god stops the flood and restores the world. Only the guilty individual is punished—in a way that perfectly suits his crime.

THE FIRST PEOPLE AND THE FLOOD

In the long-ago time, Obassi Osaw and Obassi Nai made the world together. When it was done, Obassi Nai decided to live there. Obassi Osaw went to live in the sky. Often he looked down on the world that he and Obassi Nai had made. It was beautiful, but strangely empty.

Obassi Osaw decided to make people to live there. He created man and woman, Etim Ne and Ejaw. He taught them the things they would need to know to live in the world: how to plant and hunt and find shelter for themselves. Then he placed them on the new-made earth.

Etim Ne and Ejaw set to work doing the things that Obassi Osaw had taught them. It was a fine world the gods had made, with all manner of interesting things upon it.

There was just one problem. Nowhere in all the world could Etim Ne and Ejaw find water. "We certainly can't live without it," said Etim Ne. "I will talk to Obassi Osaw."

And so he did. When Etim Ne had explained the problem, Obassi Osaw placed seven clear stones into a hollow gourd. "Make a small hole in the earth," he said, "and put one stone into it."

Etim Ne did as he was told. He made the hole and pushed the stone into it. At once, clear, sweet water gushed from the ground. It flowed and it flowed until it had formed a wide lake.

Etim Ne and Ejaw lived on the shore of that lake for

many years. They had seven sons and seven daughters. The children grew strong and healthy. When they married and had children of their own, Etim Ne gave each family a river to make its land fruitful.

Three of Etim Ne's sons did not take care of the gifts they had been given. They were neither good hunters nor diligent farmers. They would not listen when Etim Ne tried to talk to them.

Etim Ne thought long and hard and finally decided what he must do: He took away the rivers he had given to these three sons. The sons begged and pleaded with Etim Ne. What would their families do without water? How would they survive? They promised to do better, if only Etim Ne would give back their rivers.

Etim Ne relented and did as they asked. True to their word, the three sons did do better.

And so life was good. The grandchildren grew. When they were old enough to start new families, Etim Ne called them all together. He told them each to take a stone from their parents' rivers. They should plant those stones to make new rivers.

"But there is a warning," said Etim Ne. "Take care to space out the plantings so there will be enough water everywhere."

The grandchildren went forth like planters sowing seeds. They placed their stones and rivers came forth—crystal rivers that flowed through a greening countryside.

One grandson grew tired of this work. "It's too much trouble and it doesn't make sense," he told himself. So he went to his parents' river and took a basketful of stones, then emptied them all in one corner of his farm.

The waters came. They gushed and frothed. They rose and swelled. They drowned the bad grandson's fields and

knocked over his house. From all over the countryside, families ran to Etim Ne, begging him to stop the flood.

This Etim Ne could not do; it was beyond his power. With the flood waters rising and the end of everything in sight, Etim Ne prayed to Obassi Osaw.

Obassi Osaw heard the prayer and stopped the flood. He turned back the waters until there was land where land should be and water where water should be. Everyone got their farms back, except for the bad grandson. His land was at the bottom of a huge new lake, and there it would stay. This was Obassi Osaw's punishment for the young farmer.

Etim Ne called all his children and grandchildren to him. He gave them two tasks: to name all the rivers and lakes left after the flood, and to remember him as the bringer of water to the world.

Two days later, Etim Ne died in peace. The water-bringer's work was done.

QUESTIONS AND ANSWERS

Q: *When Etim Ne and Ejaw first came to Earth they found no water. What did Etim Ne do?*

A: He asked the sky god, Obassi Osaw, for water and received a gourd with seven clear stones inside. Following Obassi Osaw's instructions, Etim Ne planted one of the stones and made a lake.

Q: *When Etim Ne's children married, what did he give to each family?*

A: Etim Ne gave each family a river of its own. Thus, they had water enough for all their needs.

Q: *When three of Etim Ne's sons behaved badly, how did he punish them?*

A: He took away their rivers until they promised to mend their ways.

Q: *What did Etim Ne tell his grandchildren to do?*

A: He told them to take seven stones each from their parents' rivers and plant them. He warned the grandchildren not to plant their stones too closely together, but to spread them out so there would be water everywhere.

Q: *What caused the flood that almost destroyed the world?*

A: One of Etim Ne's grandsons did not follow instructions. Instead of taking seven stones, he took a basketful and dumped all the stones in the same place. The waters came gushing out and spread over everything.

Q: *How was the flood stopped?*

A: When Etim Ne saw what was happening, he prayed to Obassi Osaw. For Etim Ne's sake, he stopped the waters and restored the land.

Q: *Who was punished for the flood, and how?*

A: Obassi Osaw did not punish all the people for the wrongdoing of one man. He punished the disobedient grandson by leaving his land submerged underwater. The grandson lost his farm, and the rest of the people received a beautiful new lake.

EXPERT COMMENTARY

In some traditions, the Great Flood is not caused by gods or human beings. It is part of the universal order and beyond anyone's control. Mythologist Joseph Campbell explained:

> According to many . . . mythologies . . . a world flood occurs . . . at the [end] of every aeon. In India, the number of years of an aeon . . . [is] 4,320,000,000. . . . There is no question of punishment or guilt implied in a mythology . . . of this kind. Everything is completely automatic and in the sweet nature of things.[1]

This cosmic flood represents destruction and rebirth on a universal scale. African myths tend to be more grounded in human experience. John S. Mbiti discusses the process of "mythologizing" these experiences in his book on African religions:

> Myths occur in different parts of the continent, like the Niger, Zambezi and Congo [rivers] drainage basins, telling of great floods in [ancient] days, which caused destruction of mankind and animals. No doubt the annual flooding of these great rivers has in the past caused much damage to human life and property, as well as to the animals of the forest. Such damage has been incorporated into the mythology of the peoples concerned, and has survived through the centuries.[2]

Beneath their many differences, flood myths share one important feature: They do not end with destruction, but with renewal—or at least the hope of it. Mythologist Clyde W. Ford says that the flood myth becomes the story of "the death and resurrection of the world; for the water that drowns the world is also the [water] of its rebirth."[3]

3

THE GIFT OF FIRE

THE CHAGA OF TANZANIA

Somewhere, maybe 400,000 years ago, primitive cave dwellers learned to kindle fire. Like many other things in the natural world, fire could be helpful or deadly. It could give light and warmth. It could cook food, turn water to steam, and reduce piles of rubbish to ashes. Fire could also kill. It could rage over the land, burning everything in sight.

Perhaps the strangest thing about fire was the way it blazed into being, burned with bright, dancing flames, then vanished, leaving nothing of itself behind. Ashes were the remains of whatever the fire had burned, not fire itself. It was a mystery, and mystery is the beginning of myth.

Cultures all over the world have stories about the fire-bringer, a god or other being who gives humankind the gift of fire. Perhaps the best known of the fire-bringers is Prometheus, from Greek mythology. Prometheus was an outsider among the gods of Olympus. He belonged to the older group of gods known as the Titans. When the gods of Olympus withheld fire from humankind, Prometheus stole it and took it to Earth.

The !Kung (see Chapter 5) of Namibia and Botswana do not begin with gods or even people with superhuman powers. They begin with an ordinary man called Kai Kini. He is the only person in the world to have the secret of fire until the hero Gaolna comes along.

Gaolna sees Kai Kini using magic fire sticks to cook his food. This cooked food tastes much better than raw food, so Gaolna thinks that all people should have it. He grabs the fire sticks and runs, breaking off pieces and throwing them all over the world. Thus, the fire that once belonged only to Kai Kini now belongs to everyone.

This story is unusual because it does not involve a god

or god-like figure. Instead, human beings are the fire-bringers. An even more unusual fire-bringer story comes from the Chaga of Tanzania and Kenya. Not only is their fire-bringer a human being, but he takes the gift of fire up to the gods—who had not yet discovered it for themselves.

THE GIFT OF FIRE

Murile had grown tired of his life at home. His mother nagged, his brothers pestered, and Murile wanted nothing more than to get away from all of it. One day he borrowed a stool that had been in his father's family for longer than anyone could remember.

Murile took the stool outside and sat upon it. Quietly, then louder and louder, Murile sang a magic song. The stool trembled beneath him.

Murile kept singing, his voice growing stronger as the stool began to rise into the air. Up and up it went, making Murile breathless with its rising. Below on the ground, Murile's brothers saw him and started to yell. His mother came out from the house and tried to call him back.

Murile did not listen to any of them. "Take me to the heaven country, Stool," he said, and so it did.

The stool took Murile up past the tallest trees, up past the clouds, up and up until he came to the moon. The first people Murile saw there were gathering wood.

"Please," he asked politely, "Could you tell me how to get to the moon-chief's village?"

"Help us gather sticks and we will send you on your way," said one of the workers.

So Murile picked up a bundle of sticks. True to their word, the wood-gatherers directed him to some people cutting grass. Once more he asked for directions to the moon-chief's village. Once more the people promised to help if he would first do some work for them.

When Murile had cut some grass, he was directed to a group of women hoeing. Again, he worked and again he was directed to another group. He worked with herders, harvesters, gatherers, and water-carriers. Each set of directions brought him closer to his goal, until at last he arrived at the village of the moon-chief.

People were just sitting down to eat. To Murile's surprise, all their food was raw. Thinking that perhaps this was some custom of the moon folk, he asked why the food was not cooked.

The people looked at him strangely. "What is this 'cooking'?" one of them asked.

And so Murile learned that the moon folk knew nothing of fire. Seeing this as an opportunity, he went straight to the moon-chief.

"If I show you how to kindle fire and make delicious food, what will you give me?" he asked.

"We will give you cattle and sheep and goats," replied the moon-chief.

It seemed a fair bargain, so Murile agreed. He sent some of the villagers to get wood. When they did, he took the moon-chief behind the house, where no one else could see what he was about to do.

Quickly, Murile cut two sticks, one flat and the other pointed. He twirled the pointed stick between his hands until he got a spark, which he used to set fire to a patch of dry grass.

Murile began to cook. He roasted yams sweet in their skins and hot meat dripping with juices.

The moon-chief ate heartily. When he was through, he licked his lips and his fingers. "You spoke truly," he told Murile. "This food is indeed delicious."

He called all the people together and showed them the wonderful foods Murile had cooked. "This is a great man who comes to us from a far country," he said. "We must pay him well for his fire."

The villagers brought cattle and sheep and goats, and Murile became a rich man. His flocks and herds grew. He married many wives and fathered many children. And always he was honored as the bringer of fire to the people of the heaven country.

For many years, Murile was happy with his life, but at heart he remained a mortal. He began missing the home he had once scorned. So it was that one day he took leave of his friends and his wives. With his sons and his flocks and his herds, he set off on the long journey home.

There he was welcomed as a returning hero by the family that had thought him dead. There he lived for many years. And there he died.

QUESTIONS AND ANSWERS

Q: *How did Murile journey to the heaven country?*

A: He flew on a magic stool that lifted him into the sky.

Q: *Why did Murile work for the people who gave him directions?*

A: It was a fair exchange for the information Murile wanted.

Q: *How did Murile realize that the moon people did not know about fire?*

A: He saw them eating their food raw. When he asked why the food was not cooked, he discovered that the moon people had no idea what he meant.

Q: *What did the moon-chief promise Murile in return for the secret of fire?*

A: The moon-chief promised to give Murile sheep, goats, and cattle.

Q: *Why was Murile an unusual fire-bringer?*

A: Because he was a human being who took fire up into the heavens rather than a god who brought it down to Earth.

EXPERT COMMENTARY

Learning to kindle and control fire was a turning point in human development. Mythologist Joseph Campbell discusses its significance as an historic event and as a mythological theme:

> One of the earliest signs of a separation of human from animal consciousness may be seen in man's domestication of fire . . . . When this domestication occurred, we do not know; but we do know that as early as 400,000 B.C. fires were being kindled and [kept alive] in the caves of Peking man . . . . We have from all over the world innumerable myths of the capturing of fire . . . . [It] is usual in these myths to represent the separation of mankind from the beasts as having followed upon that [basic] adventure.[1]

The story of Murile may well be the only fire-bringer myth in which a human takes fire to the gods. This difference is more than just a clever plot device. As Clyde W. Ford, director of the Institute of African Mythology, points out, it changes the whole relationship between humankind and the gods:

> When . . . Prometheus stole fire from heaven . . . Zeus was angered because fire . . . was supposed to belong to no one but the gods . . . . Murile's story [gives] two different mythologies . . . about the relationship between humanity and [the gods]. The Promethean way holds that humankind is not by nature divine and must receive . . . the immortal flame . . . from the gods. The Chaga way holds that humanity is by nature divine [and has] the spark of that immortal flame already within . . . .[2]

In addition to myths about fire and fire-bringers, most African cultures have rituals involving fire. These ceremonies often involve extinguishing "old fire" for "new fire." In *The Golden Bough*, Sir James Frazer described a typical ceremony in the Sudan:

In the [Sudan] all the fires in the villages are put out and the ashes removed from the houses on the day which precedes the New Year festival. At the beginning of the new year, a new fire is lit by the friction of wood in the great straw hut where the village elders lounge away the sultry hours together; and every man takes . . . a burning brand with which he rekindles the fire on his [home] hearth.[3]

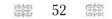

4

WHY PEOPLE GROW
OLD AND DIE

THE KONO OF SIERRA LEONE

Every culture has myths about death. In some, death is a god's punishment for disobedience. In others, it comes by mistake, jealousy, trickery, or through the evil intentions of a god or some other creature.

In African mythologies, death often comes because of a failed message. This theme is so common in Africa that "the failed message" is a mythological category of its own.[1] It begins with a god sending two animal messengers to humankind: one with a message of life, the other with a message of death.

A story from the Tonga people of Malawi is typical of the failed message pattern. The high god, Chiuta, chose a lizard and a chameleon as his messengers. Lizard carried the message that people would die and that would be the end of them. Chameleon's message promised that people would die, but would return to life. Because Lizard was naturally faster than Chameleon, he arrived first and delivered his message to the people.

The people accepted this message as the will of Chiuta. By the time Chameleon arrived with the message of life, it was too late. Lizard's message had been delivered and accepted. Humanity's fate was sealed.

In another type of failed message story, death becomes permanent because the word of the gods is wrongly spoken. In some traditions, an animal messenger makes the mistake. In others, it is a human being who speaks incorrectly. For example, in one story a man is supposed to say, "man die and come back again, moon die and stay away" whenever someone is buried. When he turns the message around—"moon die and come back again, man die and stay away"—he dooms humanity to death from which there is no return.

Failed-message stories usually involve a mistake rather than malice, or evil intent. Chameleon did not mean to be slower than Lizard. The man did not mean to get his words twisted. The disaster happens, but there is no one to blame for it.

African mythologies do have their share of evil characters. For example, in some failed-message stories the messenger deliberately twists the message. There are also stories in which death comes to humankind because of misdeeds such as trickery, deceit, hatred, or theft.

This story, "Why People Grow Old and Die," not only explains how death came to humankind, but also how the despised snake came to symbolize, or represent, renewal and endless youth.

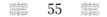

WHY PEOPLE GROW OLD AND DIE

Yataa was pleased with the people he had made. Man and Woman were handsome indeed, and worthy builders of the new world he had given them. In the course of time, they had a son—a fine, sturdy little fellow with bright eyes and winning ways. Yataa was even more pleased than before. He decided to give the new family a gift: something special, something wonderful, something that only a god could give.

Yataa decided to give them life forever. He had to think about how best to do this. He wanted to keep his people strong and handsome throughout their endless lives. Already he could see that this would not be a easy thing to do.

The people always seemed to be having accidents: running into this, tripping over that, stumbling and sometimes falling. In time, their beautiful bodies would be scarred with living. The years would add wrinkles to the scars, and Yataa's people would be a sorry sight indeed. The more Yataa thought about this problem, the more he realized what his people needed: new skins.

He would give them new skins to put on when the old ones wore out. Yataa set to work making the skins, and when he was finished, he sent for Dog. Dog came straightaway and sat at Yataa's feet.

Yataa put the skins into a package and handed the

package to him. "Dog," he said, "I want you to take this to my people. Take good care of it; it is very valuable."

Dog promised to take care of the package, and off he went on the long journey to the place where Yataa's people lived. Dog loped along at a good speed until he came to a small stream. There on its banks, several animals were eating.

"Come eat with us," said one of them, and waved something delicious in front of Dog's nose.

Dog was hungry, and the food looked tasty. He saw no harm in resting for a time, so he sat down with the group and began to eat.

"That's a fine looking package," said a snake, who had been sunning himself on a rock.

"It ought to be," Dog said proudly. "Yataa himself made it."

Everyone was impressed that Yataa's own messenger had joined their little group. They were full of questions about Yataa and what it was like to live in the household of a god.

While the others chattered, Snake stared at the package. "Yesss," he hissed, "a fine package indeed. What could be inside such a fine package?"

"New skins to make Yataa's people young again," said Dog. He saw no harm in telling this to such a friendly group of animals.

Snake behaved strangely. At first, he fairly twitched with interest, then he began to yawn. He curled up on his rock and yawned and yawned. Soon all the other animals were yawning. Dog was yawning too, and he began to fall asleep.

That was Dog's big mistake, for Snake had only been pretending to be sleepy. When he had lulled the other

animals to sleep, he took Yataa's package and slithered away.

Dog was so heartbroken that he sat howling into the afternoon sky. So it was, and so it always would be. Not even Yataa himself could change it. To this day, snakes can put on new skins and become young again, while humans must grow old and die.

QUESTIONS AND ANSWERS

Q: *Why did Yataa want to give his people a gift?*

A: Yataa was proud of his creations. He wanted to show this pride by giving people the most wonderful gift he could bestow: the ability to renew their youth and live forever.

Q: *How did Yataa decide to give his people this gift?*

A: He made them new skins to use when the old ones began to wear out.

Q: *What was Dog's job?*

A: He was a messenger sent by Yataa to deliver the skins to humans. Yataa chose Dog for this important job because he was a faithful servant.

Q: *Why did Dog stop along the way?*

A: Because he was hungry and a group of animals invited him to eat with them. He saw no harm in stopping, so he put Yataa's package beside him where he could keep an eye on it.

Q: *Why were the animals so impressed with Dog?*

A: Because he was Yataa's own messenger and could tell them about life in the household of a god. They asked endless questions, most of which seemed to be entirely innocent.

Q: *Why did Snake become interested in the package?*

A: Because it was well made—"a fine looking package"—and came from Yataa himself. Snake reasoned that it must be something of great importance and determined to find out what it was.

Q: *How did Snake get the package away from Dog?*

A: He lulled Dog and the other animals to sleep by pretending to yawn. When Dog's eyes closed, Snake grabbed the package and ran away.

Q: *What happened because of this theft?*

A: Snakes acquired the ability to shed their old skins and grow new ones. This made them a symbol of immortality, or endless life. Humans had to go through life in their same old skins and then die because they could not renew themselves.

EXPERT COMMENTARY

The snake is perhaps the most unloved creature in the world. It is also one of the most familiar characters in mythology. Almost every tradition has a good stock of stories about snakes, or serpents as they are also called.

A Dictionary of Symbols discusses some of the things the snake symbolizes:

> Because it sheds its skin, it symbolizes resurrection. Because of its [gliding] movement it signifies strength. Because of its viciousness, it represents the evil side of nature. Its ability to shed its skin greatly impressed ancient writers: Philo of Alexandria believed that when the snake shakes off its skin it likewise shakes off its old age . . . .[2]

The idea of "temporary" death is more common than straightforward immortality (never dying). Dying and returning treats death as part of the endless cycles of nature. This is the "renewal" symbolized by the snake shedding its skin. Mythologist Joseph Campbell called this process the myth of eternal return:

> The myth of eternal return . . . displays an order of fixed forms that appear and reappear through all time. The daily round of the sun, the waning and waxing moon, the cycle of the year, and the rhythm of . . . birth, death and new birth, represent a miracle of continuous [renewal] that is [part of] the nature of the universe.[3]

5

HOW BABOONS
BECAME MONKEYS

THE !KUNG OF THE KALAHARI, SOUTHERN AFRICA

The !Kung people are an ancient group of hunter-gatherers. Once they roamed the arid Kalahari in small, extended family groups. Rarely, if ever, were there more than thirty people in these groups. They had no chiefs, no police, no formal laws, and no jails. Clock time meant nothing to them. They timed their lives by the cycles of nature.

The !Kung are part of a group known as the San. They speak a language that sounds odd to outsiders because it uses "clicks" made with the tongue against the roof of the mouth. An exclamation point stands for this sound, which is why the group name is written as "!Kung" in English.

!Kung mythology deals with the basic facts of existence: the origin of humankind, the coming of death, the behavior of animals, and the cycles of life. It has its share of fantastic creatures, such as rain beasts, monstrous serpents, witches, wizards, and magicians.

Many !Kung tales show a strong sense of right and wrong: Bad deeds are usually punished and good deeds are rewarded. For example, nine young girls are cruel to an old magician, who turns them into willow trees. A tenth girl, who did not join with the others, is spared.

Such transformation stories are common in mythologies all over the world. People are changed into every imaginable form, from stars and mountains to bugs and reptiles. As in the tale of the magician and the willow trees, transformation is often a form of punishment.

Stories often begin with an angry or jealous god striking at someone or something that has offended him. They may also involve a curse or forbidden behavior. For example, in

Greek mythology anyone who looked at the fearsome monster Medusa would immediately turn to stone.

There are also people or creatures that can transform themselves at will. They are called metamorphs, or shape-shifters. For example, the praying mantis, or *kaggen* as the !Kung know him, can appear as an insect, an animal, or a human being. He is called by many names and given many attributes, or characteristics.

In some stories, he is the world creator. In others, he is a trickster, doing outrageous things. In all his forms and roles he can transform other creatures and even create new ones.

In the story here called "How Baboons Became Monkeys," Kaggen appears in his human form as a hunter. This binds him to a certain code.

Ancient hunters did not kill in anger; they killed only for food. The hunt became an elaborate ritual, which connected the hunter to his prey. Together, the hunter and the hunted played a role in the endless cycle of life and death.

Without this ritual relationship, the !Kung and other African tribes regarded killing as an act of murder. This meant that Kaggen could not kill the people who killed his only son. But he did not have to let them go free, either. Because of his powers, Kaggen found a punishment that truly suited the crime.

HOW BABOONS BECAME MONKEYS

Long ago, baboons were not monkeys, but little people. They were a quarrelsome bunch, always making trouble of one kind or another. One day, they saw a young !Kung boy roaming through the bush. They recognized him at once—he was Cogaz, son of the hunter, Kaggen.

The baboons did not like Kaggen. He was the finest hunter in the land, and they were jealous of him. They were also afraid of him.

The baboons amused themselves by hatching evil plots against Kaggen. Each plot was meaner than the one before, but each was nothing but empty words . . . until the day the baboons saw Cogaz alone in the bush. They were not afraid of a little boy. They watched Cogaz with bright, eager eyes.

Cogaz was collecting sticks for his father to make into hunting bows. He did this task the way his father did things, earnestly and with complete attention to his work. The baboons surrounded Cogaz before he noticed what was happening.

They mocked and jeered, grabbing at Cogaz and snatching away his sticks. "Your father thinks he's so smart . . . the mighty hunter. Wants to kill us, you know. Oh yes . . . wants to kill us dead, dead, dead . . . ."

One of the baboons pinched Cogaz. Another tweaked his nose.

"Stop that!" Cogaz shouted, and tried to push the little men away. "My father is a hunter; a hunter kills only for food."

The baboons roared with laughter. "So Kaggen wants to eat us? For shame!"

Cogaz tried to explain, but the baboons were in no mood to listen. They danced around Cogaz, moving faster and faster. They whooped and screamed. "We also are great hunters, young Cogaz . . . just look, we've caught *you*."

With that, the baboons fell upon Cogaz and killed him. Then they tied his body up in the top of a tree. They began to dance around the tree, singing of their victory.

The instant Cogaz died, Kaggen woke suddenly from his afternoon nap. Something was wrong! He could feel it in the air. The sky above was blue and clear; the earth below was warm. There was no sign of fire or storm, no sound of dangerous animals prowling the bush. Still, something was wrong.

"Bring my magic charms," Kaggen shouted to his wife.

Kaggen rubbed himself with magic and sat very still. Pictures formed in his mind. Soon, he knew what the baboons had done to Cogaz. He jumped to his feet and hurried away to find them.

They were still dancing and singing when Kaggen arrived. When they saw him they grew afraid and clapped their hands over their mouths.

"No!" Kaggen told them. "Sing as before. I want to hear it."

The baboons were too frightened to disobey, and so they sang.

"And dance again, too," Kaggen ordered. "Dance as if your lives depended upon it, and do not stop until I tell you."

Again, the baboons were frightened, and so they danced. They danced and they sang, and as Kaggen

watched them, he decided what to do. He slipped away and got a basket filled with pegs.

When he returned to the tree, the baboons were still dancing. Their small feet raised great clouds of dust as they stomped and whirled.

Swiftly and quietly, Kaggen slipped behind the dancing men and drove a peg into each one's backside. Where Kaggen put the pegs, tails grew. Instead of singing, the baboons began to bark and babble, making yak-yak-yakking noises in harsh, frantic voices. They bounded away, leaping and barking as they ran.

When they were gone, Kaggen climbed the tree and brought Cogaz down. With his magic charms, he made Cogaz live again, and the two of them went home.

As for the baboons—they were men no longer. They had become monkeys. They live in the wild to this day, eating beetles and worms, scratching fleas, and chattering among themselves. It is said that only the !Kung can understand what they are trying to say.

QUESTIONS AND ANSWERS

Q: *Why did the baboons hate Kaggen?*

A: They were jealous and afraid of him because he was a skilled hunter.

Q: *At first, what did the baboons do about their hatred for Kaggen? Why?*

A: They grumbled and plotted among themselves. They hatched many schemes but were too afraid to carry them out.

Q: *Why did they attack Kaggen's son, Cogaz?*

A: Because they saw an opportunity when they encountered Cogaz so far from his father's protection. Although they feared a mighty hunter, they were not afraid of a little boy.

Q: *What did the baboons do to Cogaz?*

A: They killed him and hung his body in a tree, then danced around it.

Q: *How did Kaggen learn what had happened to Cogaz?*

A: Kaggen had powers that the baboons did not understand. He woke suddenly from sleep, feeling that something was wrong. He used his magic to find out what it was.

Q: *Why would a hunter like Kaggen refuse to kill the people who killed his son?*

A: Because ancient hunters were bound by a code. They killed only for food—never in anger.

Q: *How did Kaggen turn the baboons into monkeys?*

A: He made them dance around the tree and drove pegs into their backsides. The pegs became tails, and soon the baboons were fully transformed into monkeys who ran off into the hills.

Q: *What did Kaggen do for his son?*

A: He used his magic to restore Cogaz to life.

EXPERT COMMENTARY

Even before they were changed, the baboons seemed to behave more like monkeys than human beings. Their new form showed what they are actually like inside. According to classics professor Joseph B. Solodow, this is common in transformation stories:

> [M]etamorphosis [transformation] . . . is a process by which characteristics of a person . . . are given physical [expression] and so are [made] visible . . . . Metamorphosis makes plain a person's qualities, yet without passing judgment on them.[1]

This idea of transformation showing inner qualities applies only to the baboons, who were changed once and for all by an outside force. Unlike them, Kaggen is a true shape-shifter. He can change to any form at any time.

Kaggen's shape-shifting stands for what Clyde W. Ford calls "the transformative [possibilities] of life."[2] As Ford points out, myths about Kaggen:

> often reveal him either shape-shifting into other animals or creating other animals out of nothing. When not involved in these [actions], Mantis [Kaggen] transforms back into an ordinary human, a San [!Kung] who must go about life's daily tasks.[3]

The hunter's code transforms the taking of life into participation in the endless cycle of birth and death. Mythologist Joseph Campbell explained:

> Man lives by killing, and there is a sense of guilt connected with that . . . . Early hunters usually had a kind of animal divinity [god]—the technical name would be the animal master, the animal who is the master animal. The animal master sends the flocks to be killed . . . the basic hunting myth is . . . a kind of [agreement] between the animal world and the human world. The animal gives its life

willingly, with the understanding that its life transcends [rises above] its physical [body] and will be returned to the soil . . . through some ritual of restoration.[4]

Some cultures draw an outline of the animal in the dirt and pour a portion of its blood onto it. Thus, the animal is literally "returned to the soil."

6

HOW ANANSI GOT
GOD'S STORIES

THE ASHANTI OF GHANA

Trickster gods appear in mythologies all over the world. Some stories about them may be funny or outrageous, but the trickster is not a comedian. He is a "contrary"—he goes against the established social order, breaks the rules, and generally creates confusion wherever he goes. As mythologist Harold Courlander put it, the trickster represents "chance, accident, and unpredictability."[1]

Not only is the trickster well aware of his role, but he also enjoys it. If he is caught by the victims of his schemes, he rarely apologizes for what he has done. For example, the Yoruban trickster Eshu decided one day, for no particular reason, to break up a lifelong friendship between two farmers.

Every day he walked the path between their two fields, wearing a black hat. One day, he wore a hat that was white on one side and red on the other. He walked through the fields as usual, careful that each farmer would see only one side of the hat and think it to be that color all around.

The two men began to fight, arguing over whether Eshu wore a red hat or a white one. When the situation got out of hand, Eshu calmly admitted what he had done: "Sowing discord (conflict)," he added, "is my greatest delight."[2]

Although the trickster's stunts can be cruel and mean-spirited, he is not completely evil. He disrupts the normal order of things. Sometimes this actually turns out to be beneficial. Even positive changes can bring a certain amount of disorganization and uncertainty. Through his bold deeds, the trickster often becomes a culture hero. Prometheus, the Greek god who stole fire and gave it to humans, was a trickster figure. So was Kaggen, the mantis, who created the world and taught the !Kung the ways of the hunt.

Anansi the spider is the trickster figure of the Ashanti and other tribes of the Akan cultural group. He has a knack for finding the weaknesses of other creatures and using them to his own advantage. He generally used this talent to create mischief and mayhem. But in one story, he uses it to bring a wonderful gift to humankind.

HOW ANANSI GOT GOD'S STORIES

Nyankophon, the sky god, owned all the stories in the world. Many had tried to buy them, but failed to meet Nyankophon's price. Then, along came Anansi the spider.

"I want the stories," he said, "and I will pay whatever you ask." Nyankophon only laughed, but Anansi would not be put off. Again and again he asked the price, until Nyankophon threw up his hands.

"All right, then, this is my price—bring me Onini the python, Mmoboro the hornet swarm, Osebo the leopard, and Mmoatia the nature spirit. Can you do that, Spider, or shall we forget the whole thing?"

"I'll bring you all of them, you will see," said Anansi, and bid Nyankophon a good day.

Anansi scurried home to gather the things he would need. He cut a long branch from the tree by his door and gathered some sturdy vines. Then he asked his wife, Aso, to come with him.

Into the jungle Anansi and Aso went. When they saw Onini curled in the branches of his favorite tree, they began to shout at one another.

"He's shorter, I tell you!" screamed Aso.

"Foolish woman! Onini is so long he could swallow this puny branch whole."

And so it went, with Anansi and Aso raising such a ruckus that birds flew from the trees and small animals scurried for their burrows. Onini raised his head and demanded to know why Anansi and Aso had disturbed his nap.

When they explained their argument, the great python unwrapped himself from the tree, and in one graceful motion, slid to the ground. "This is easy enough to settle," he said, and told Anansi to lay the branch down. He stretched himself alongside it.

Now Anansi knew that Onini took great pride in being the biggest, the longest, and the best of everything. Anansi paced back and forth, shaking his head and making tsk-tsking noises. "Maybe you really are shorter, Onini," he said. "Can you stretch out more?"

Onini stretched and stretched. He stretched until he could stretch no more. Quick as anything, Anansi wrapped the vine around Onini's body, just under the head. "This will keep you from slipping," he explained, and then told Aso to pull hard on Onini's tail.

While Aso pulled, Anansi wrapped. Onini was so busy trying to stretch himself that he did not notice anything until it was over. He was bound fast. That was just like a python. They were big and strong, but not terribly bright.

"Well, now," said Anansi, "it seems I can take my first payment to Nyankophon."

On the way home, Anansi was already thinking about Mmoboro, the hornet swarm. He hollowed out a large gourd and filled it with water. Then he found a big palm leaf. With these things, he approached the swarm. He climbed the tree and worked his way up behind the nest. Then quick as anything, he poured half the water in the gourd on himself and the other half on the hornets.

The hornets, having been thoroughly doused, woke with a furious humming. Anansi held the palm leaf over himself and the swarm. "Hornets, oh hornets," he called, "the sky is pouring rain. Maybe you should move into this gourd to wait out the storm. I can keep you sheltered with this leaf while you come over."

There was another buzzing, and then the swarm rose in a single body and moved into the gourd. Quickly, Anansi clapped the palm leaf over the opening to hold the hornets inside. He smiled to himself. One thing about hornets: What one did, all did. The whole swarm was buzzing unhappily in Anansi's gourd.

"Well, now," said Anansi, "it seems I can take my second payment to Nyankophon."

For Osebo the leopard, Anansi dug a deep pit in the path between Osebo's lair and the watering hole. He covered it with leaves and sticks, then ran away.

The next morning, Anansi returned with two thick branches and one heavy rock. He looked into the pit, and there was Osebo, pacing around and around.

"Osebo," said Anansi, "What are you doing in that hole?"

"Never mind that," snarled Osebo. "Just get me out!"

"Will you promise not to eat me if I do?" asked Anansi.

"I am Osebo the leopard. I promise nothing to anyone," came the reply. "Now do as I say."

Anansi did not argue. He put the branches across the opening of the pit and told Osebo to put his front paws over them. When Osebo did so, Anansi hit him in the head with the rock.

That was the way of things with leopards. They expected everybody to be afraid of them, even when they were the ones trapped in the pit. "Well, now," said Anansi, "it seems I can take my third payment to Nyankophon."

For Mmoatia the nature spirit, Anansi made a wooden doll and coated it with sticky tree sap. He attached two strings to its head; one for nodding *yes*, the other for shaking *no*. Then with a bowl of his wife's tastiest mashed

yams, he went to the spring where the nature spirits liked to play. He set the doll and the yams in a place where he could hide to work the strings. Then he waited.

Mmoatia came dancing, flitting here and there. She stopped when she saw the yams. "Oh, they look delicious. May I have some?"

The doll nodded *yes*. When Mmoatia took a step toward the bowl, the doll shook its head *no*.

Mmoatia scowled and tapped her foot. "You changed your mind?"

Anansi, who was by now thoroughly enjoying this escapade, pulled the *yes* string.

"Now that's rude," said Mmoatia. "Will you at least tell me why?"

Anansi pulled the *no* string.

"Well!" Mmoatia jumped at the doll and slapped it across the face. Her hand stuck. Mmoatia slapped the other cheek and that hand stuck, too. Mmoatia squealed. In a rage, she kicked at the doll and her feet stuck; butted with her head and that stuck. She screamed and wiggled, but none of it helped a bit. That was one thing about nature spirits; they could throw magnificent tantrums.

"Well, now," said Anansi, "it seems I am finally ready for Nyankophon."

So it was that Anansi the spider handed Nyankophon a sticky mess of wooden doll and enraged nature spirit. "I think this fills my part of the bargain," said Anansi.

Nyankophon threw back his head and laughed heartily. "Indeed it does, Spider. I never thought you would do it, but you certainly have. I congratulate you. The stories are yours."

So this is how Anansi came to own all the stories in the world. He gladly shares them with humankind. He asks only that anyone who tells a story acknowledge that Anansi the spider is its true and rightful owner.

QUESTIONS AND ANSWERS

Q: *What did Nyankophon think when Anansi first asked to buy his stories?*

A: Nyankophon thought that Anansi would never be able to meet his price. Many had tried and failed; he did not expect the spider to do any better.

Q: *Why did the python allow himself to be measured?*

A: The python was eager to prove that he was the biggest and strongest in the land.

Q: *Why did the hornets fly into Anansi's gourd?*

A: Anansi tricked the hornets into believing there was a hard rain. He poured water on himself to make his words more convincing.

Q: *How did Anansi know that all the hornets would fly into his gourd?*

A: Because the swarm acted as one. In many circumstances, the swarm was fearsome and even deadly because it acted as a group. In this case, their strength became a weakness because there was no one individual to question Anansi's statements.

Q: *Why did the leopard refuse to make a promise to Anansi?*

A: The leopard was powerful and fierce. Even in the pit, he considered himself stronger than Anansi. It did not occur to him that, at that moment, Anansi's strength was greater than his own.

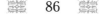

Q: *Why did the nature spirit become angry with Anansi's doll?*

A: The nature spirit believed that the doll was being deliberately rude to her.

Q: *What do Anansi's dealings with the python, the hornet swarm, the leopard, and the nature spirit have in common?*

A: They all involved tricks that worked because they played on some weakness or peculiarity of each character. Anansi had a talent for spotting and using these "quirks."

EXPERT COMMENTARY

The spider is a popular trickster figure in many African and non-African cultures. For example, in the United States, the Sioux people have Iktomi. Like Anansi, Iktomi is the subject of hundreds of tales. Joseph Epes Brown, a teacher of American Indian religions, discussed the qualities of the spider:

> You appreciate why the spider was chosen if you look at all the different types of spiders and what they are able to do, and how superior they are as hunters, and . . . how spiders that build their webs in . . . circles are able to draw out of their own being two different kinds of threads, one smooth and one sticky . . . and of course it is the sticky ones that catch the prey.[3]

The duality, or two-sidedness, of the trickster is a basic part of his character. Many characters in mythology can be classified as either "good" or "bad." The trickster, however, is both. He defies classification, as mythologist Joseph Campbell explains:

> This . . . curiously fascinating figure of the trickster appears to have been the chief mythological character of the paleolithic [Stone Age] world of story. A fool, and a cruel . . . cheat, an [extreme example] of the principle of disorder, he is nevertheless the culture-bringer also . . . . In the paleolithic sphere from which this figure [comes], he was the [original pattern] of the hero, the giver of all great boons— the fire-bringer and the teacher of mankind.[4]

When the trickster plays the hero or the culture-bringer, he does it in his own outlandish way. His motives may be good, but his methods are usually deceptive or dishonest. When his motives are bad, he can do outrageous and terrible things without a pang of conscience. As Dr. Scott

Leonard points out, this makes the trickster's world very much like the one humankind actually inhabits:

> In trickster tales, [the] innocent are as likely to suffer as the guilty . . . . The world is sometimes far more [changeable and uncertain] than we would like to admit; bad things do happen to innocent people, the greedy often do win the day.[5]

7

KWASI BENEFO
IN THE
LAND OF THE DEAD

THE ASHANTI OF GHANA

In many mythologies, the "land of the dead" is located somewhere under the earth. In traditional African mythologies, this underworld, as it is also called, is not usually a place of punishment. All people, good and bad alike, go there when they die.

Sometimes, living people may journey to the underworld and return, in time, to life. A common reason for visiting the underworld was to rescue a loved one. For example, the Greek poet Orpheus journeyed there to bring his wife, Eurydice, back from the dead. He begged for her life with such feeling that Hades, lord of the underworld, granted his request. There was one condition: Orpheus should not look behind him until he and Eurydice were back in the mortal world.

Orpheus made it all the way to the portal, then turned to make sure Eurydice was safely behind him. At this, she disappeared before his eyes. The grieving Orpheus went back to the mortal world, hopeless and utterly alone. In his numb sorrow, he stumbles into a frenzied ritual and is torn apart by crazed worshipers of the god Dionysus.

Greek mythology is full of such tragedies as brutal death, sad endings, and a sense of fate that is both evil and inescapable. African mythologies generally lack this sense of tragedy. They treat sadness, suffering, and death as part of life, not the result of an evil fate.

The story of Kwasi Benefo is a good example. Like Orpheus, Kwasi Benefo went to the land of the dead because he was overcome by grief. Instead of tragedy and violent death, however, he found acceptance and renewal.

KWASI BENEFO IN THE LAND OF THE DEAD

Life was good for Kwasi Benefo. His fields were green and good. He owned many cattle. In all his life, only one thing was missing: a wife to share it with him. There was in his village a young woman who pleased him, so he made arrangements for them to be married.

Kwasi Benefo was a happy man. He grew to love his young wife, and she returned his affection. Then she got sick and began to fade. In time she died. Kwasi Benefo's life became hollow. His house was silent, for he lived there alone with only his grief for company.

His family and friends began to nag him about getting on with his life. "This is the way the world is, Kwasi Benefo," they said. "People live and people die. Find another wife."

In time, Kwasi Benefo followed their advice. He went to a neighboring village and found there a young woman who pleased him. They were married, and once more Kwasi Benefo was content with his life. His wife managed his home with skill and was a good companion. Then came the wonderful news that she was to have a baby. Kwasi Benefo would soon become a father! But after Kwasi Benefo's wife had been pregnant for some time, she began wasting away. Before Kwasi Benefo's eyes, she grew weaker and weaker and soon died.

Kwasi Benefo could not be comforted. He stayed in his

house and saw no one. The baby inside his wife had died with her. He mourned the life that was lost and the life that never was.

The parents of Kwasi Benefo's dead wife were worried about him. He had loved their daughter well, and he was a good man. So they agreed together to offer him their other daughter as a bride.

This they did, and although Kwasi Benefo was grateful, he was not ready to marry again. The pain of his wife's death was too fresh. It was with him every day, and sometimes at night he felt her calling to him.

"That is the way it is when someone dies," said his wife's father.

"It becomes less painful in time," said her mother.

Although Kwasi Benefo could not see it then, his wife's parents were right. He worked. He lived. In time, the pain lessened, and he went to his wife's parents to talk about their younger daughter.

Once more, Kwasi Benefo was married. Once more, he was happy. And then came the greatest joy: His wife presented him with a fine son. Kwasi Benefo began to believe that his days of sorrow were truly over.

Then one day Kwasi Benefo was heading home from his fields when a neighbor woman ran toward him screaming. What she said did not make sense—something about a tree falling.

Sensible people did not get hysterical over such things. "I don't understand," said Kwasi Benefo. "Did this tree fall on my house?"

"No," said the woman, but the tone of her voice made Kwasi Benefo feel tight and cold inside. The woman wiped tears from her eyes. "We were coming home from the river. Your wife sat down to rest a moment under that tree . . . ."

Kwasi Benefo did not wait to hear more. He raced toward the village, screaming his wife's name.

There was no answer. His wife's lifeless body was laid out on her sleeping mat. Her death was so sudden and so senseless that Kwasi Benefo could not bear the pain. He gave a mighty cry and slumped to the ground as if he were dead. His neighbors summoned the medicine man.

"Kwasi Benefo is not dead," said the medicine man. "At least, his body lives. As for his spirit . . . that is another matter. That, we shall have to see about."

Kwasi Benefo woke up. He walked again, he talked again. He buried his third wife. But this time he did not return to normal. This time, he walked away from his village, his farm, and his life. He took his young son to live with his wife's parents. And he disappeared.

He went deep into the bush, where no other humans lived. He built a crude shelter and lived on roots and seeds. He wanted nothing. He cared for nothing. He passed the time.

When the years had dulled the pain, he went to a village where he was not known. There, he started to farm again and took a fourth wife. He loved her well, as he had the others. But like the others, she did not live long after marrying Kwasi Benefo.

Kwasi Benefo went back to his home village. He did not go to rebuild his farm or to marry again, but only to die.

"I want my life to end here, where it began," he told his friends. "I want to be buried near the graves of my ancestors."

So it was that Kwasi Benefo became a strange and lonely figure in the village. He lived as a shadow—a man alive yet beyond all feeling of grief or joy. He had given up hope of escaping his fate, but he still wanted to understand it. Why had these things happened to him?

Kwasi Benefo knew only one way to answer that question. He gathered a few things, bid his friends goodbye, and set out upon the journey of a lifetime. Kwasi Benefo was going to Asamando, the land of the dead.

He journeyed to a far country, to a bleak and barren land where there was a river. It was deep and fast-moving; a torrent of waters, rushing off to nowhere. Kwasi Benefo sat himself down on its banks, wondering how to get across.

A withered old crone appeared on the other side. Kwasi Benefo recognized her at once from the stories he had heard all his life. It was Amokye, who guarded the way into Asamando.

"Why have you come to this place?" she demanded. "You are a living man, not a spirit. Who are you?"

When Kwasi Benefo told Amokye his name, she nodded. "Yes. I have heard of you. Your wives all say that you are a good and kind man."

"I must see them," said Kwasi Benefo. He started to say more, to plead with Amokye, but she silenced him with a wave of her hand. Before Kwasi Benefo's eyes, the rushing waters grew still. The riverbed bulged upward, making the water shallower.

"Come then," said Amokye, and Kwasi Benefo walked across the river into Asamando. Amokye pointed out the way he should go, and when he had thanked her, Kwasi Benefo began to walk.

He walked and he walked. He walked until he was tired down in his bones, but still he walked. At last, he came to a cottage. Around the cottage, he heard the sounds of village life, but he saw nothing and no one. He heard the beloved voices of his wives, singing a song of welcome.

Inside the cottage, a bucket of water and some washcloths appeared before him. "Refresh yourself after the long journey," said one wife. When Kwasi Benefo had washed off the trail dust, a dish of food and a jug of water appeared on the table before him. "You must be hungry, dear," said the voice of another wife.

While Kwasi Benefo ate, his wives sang about the land of the living, and how happy each had been to share his life. When Kwasi Benefo finished eating, the food vanished and a sleeping mat appeared.

Kwasi Benefo laid down upon it while his wives continued to sing. The song had changed. It was no longer about what was past, but what was now. Live again, Kwasi Benefo's wives sang. Marry again; this time, his wife would not die. This time, Kwasi Benefo and his wife would have many children and share many years. This time, life would be good.

With this song ringing in his ears, Kwasi Benefo fell asleep. When he woke, he was no longer in Asamando, but on the other side of the river, which was as deep and fast-moving as before.

Kwasi Benefo went to his home village. He built a new house and married a new wife. They had many children and shared many years. Sometimes, Kwasi Benefo would smile to himself, remembering his visit to Asamando. His wives had been right. This time, life was good.

QUESTIONS AND ANSWERS

Q: *What did Kwasi Benefo's friends say after his first wife died?*

A: They said that death was the way of the world. They thought that Kwasi Benefo should remarry and get on with his life.

Q: *What new happiness did Kwasi Benefo find in his second marriage? What new sorrow?*

A: He learned that his wife was going to have a baby. He was looking forward to fatherhood, but when his wife died, so did their unborn child.

Q: *What did Kwasi Benefo's in-laws do after their daughter died?*

A: They worried that Kwasi Benefo was suffering too much. He had been a good and kind husband to their first daughter, so they decided to offer him their second daughter as a bride.

Q: *How did Kwasi Benefo respond to his in-laws' offer?*

A: At first, he turned it down. He still missed his wife, and sometimes at night, he thought he heard her calling to him. When time eased his pain, he returned to his in-laws and asked for their second daughter as a wife. They married and had a child.

Q: *How did Kwasi Benefo's third wife die? Why did he pass out when he saw her body?*

A: She died in a freak accident; she had been sitting under a large tree that fell. When Kwasi Benefo went in to see her body, he was overcome by the suddenness and senselessness of her death.

Q: *Why did Kwasi Benefo leave his home and go into the bush?*

A: He had lost the will to live. In the bush, he existed without human companionship. When he found the strength to build a new life, he went as a stranger to a new village. There he settled and got married again. The death of his fourth wife broke his spirit entirely.

Q: *Why did Kwasi Benefo journey to the land of the dead? What did he find there?*

A: Kwasi Benefo went to the land of the dead because he wanted to learn why his life had come to such grief, and why all the women who loved him had died.
In the land of the dead, he did not find clear answers to these questions, but his four wives gave him the will to go on.

EXPERT COMMENTARY

African mythology tends to focus on this life and show humankind as part of the natural world. The beliefs hold that, for all its pain and sorrow, earthly life is basically good. Teacher Camilla L. Greene writes:

> Africans are earthbound. Their lands and the earth are very real . . . . African myths . . . express joy in life and human activity . . . . Man is [shown] as completely . . . anchored in this world.[1]

When Kwasi Benefo's wives welcomed him in Asamando, they did not speak their greeting—they sang it. Singing is an important part of everyday life among the Ashanti. There are songs of greeting and songs of farewell; songs of celebration, praise, and comfort. The songs of Kwasi Benefo's wives are what Harold Courlander describes as "maiden songs":

> In Akan society, maiden songs are sung on moonlit nights by women who form themselves into little performing groups for this purpose. The women in a group stand in a circle and clap their hands as they sing. Each one takes a turn at leading the verses. The songs are used mainly for praising or making references to loved ones, brothers, or other kinsmen or outstanding men in the community.[2]

GLOSSARY

Agricultural Revolution—The beginning of grain agriculture and stock about ten to twelve thousand years ago.

Akan cultural group—A cluster of cultural groups living mainly in central Ghana.

animal master—In hunting mythology, the leader of the deathless herd.

Asamando—In Ashanti myth, the land of the dead.

Australopithecus—The first human ancestor that appeared in Africa about 4 million years ago.

contrary—Opposed; in mythology, a trickster character who violates normal social standards.

crone—A withered old woman.

divination—The act of telling the future or probing secret knowledge.

erratic—Unpredictable; straying from a set course.

eternal return—The endless cycles of life, in which birth and death play an equal part.

extended family—Family group including three or more generations of parents, siblings, their spouses, and their children.

failed-message myth—A type of African myth in which death comes into the world because a messenger from the gods arrives late or confuses the message.

fire-bringer—God or human who brings the gift of fire to humankind.

Homo sapiens—Modern humankind.

hunter-gatherers—Nomadic groups that live by hunting and foraging for food.

metamorph—A creature that can change its form at will.

Middle Passage—The route of slave ships carrying slaves from Africa to the Americas.

origin myth—Also creation myth; story of the beginning of the world or humankind.

orishas—The gods of the Yoruban people.

pantheon—All the gods of a particular cultural group.

ritual—A set form for worship or other public ceremonies.

savanna—In Africa, the grassland plains.

sub-Saharan Africa—Part of the African continent south of the Sahara desert.

transformation—A major change in form, characteristics, or behavior.

tribe—A group of people who share common ancestry, social customs, and language.

trickster—A god or mythological creature who violates social norms and often takes advantage of others. A cheat or liar.

✺ CHAPTER NOTES ✺

Preface

1. Kwame Anthony Appiah and Henry Louis Gates, Jr., ed., *Africana: The Encyclopedia of the African and African-American Experience* (New York: Basic Books, 1999), p. 1657.

2. John S. Mbiti, *African Religions and Philosophy* (Garden City, N.Y.: Anchor Books, 1970), p. 24.

3. Richard Leakey and Roger Lewin, *Origins Reconsidered: In Search of What Makes Us Human* (New York: Doubleday, 1992), Frontpiece.

4. Appiah and Gates, p. 872.

5. Britannica.com, "Africa: Migrations," 2001 <www.britannica.com/eb/print?eu=114430> (June 21, 2002).

6. BBC World Service, "Slavery," *The Story of Africa*, n.d. <http://www.bbc.co.uk/worldservice/africa/features/storyofafrica/9chapter2.shtml> (June 3, 2002).

Chapter 1. Coming Down From the Sky

1. Kwame Anthony Appiah and Henry Louis Gates, Jr., ed., *Africana: the Encyclopedia of the African and African American Experience* (New York: Basic Books, 1999), p. 2035.

2. Appiah and Gates, p. 1463.

3. Harold Courlander, *Tales of Yoruba Gods and Heroes* (New York: Fawcett Books, 1972), pp. 23–24.

4. Sandra T. Barnes, ed., *Africa's Ogun* (Bloomington, Ind.: Indiana University Press, 1989), p. 19.

Chapter 2. The First People and the Flood

1. Joseph Campbell, *Myths to Live By* (New York: Bantam Books, Inc., 1973), pp. 75–76.

2. John S. Mbiti, *African Religions and Philosophy* (Garden City, N.Y.: Anchor Books, 1970), pp. 70–71.

3. Clyde W. Ford, *The Hero With an African Face: Mythic Wisdom of Traditional Africa* (New York: Bantam Books, 1999), p. 180.

Chapter 3. The Gift of Fire

1. Joseph Campbell, *Myths to Live By* (New York: Bantam Books, Inc., 1973), p. 248.

2. Clyde W. Ford, *The Hero With an African Face: Mythic Wisdom of Traditional Africa* (New York: Bantam Books, 1999), p. 49.

3. Sir James Frazer and Theodor H. Gaster, ed., *The New Golden Bough* (abridged) (New York: New American Library, 1964), pp. 703–704.

Chapter 4. Why People Grow Old and Die

1. Clyde W. Ford, *The Hero With an African Face: Mythic Wisdom of Traditional Africa* (New York: Bantam Books, 1999), p. 193.

2. J. E. Cirlot, *A Dictionary of Symbols* (New York: Philosophical Library, 1962), p. 274.

3. Joseph Campbell, *The Masks of God: Oriental Mythology* (New York: Penguin Books, 1977), p. 3.

Chapter 5. How Baboons Became Monkeys

1. Rand Johnson, Ph.D., *Ovid: A Roman View of Myth*, n.d. <http://homepages.wmich.edu/~johnsorh/Myth/ovid1.html> (July 5, 2002).

2. Clyde W. Ford, *The Hero With an African Face: Mythic Wisdom of Traditional Africa* (New York: Bantam Books, 1999), p. 104.

3. Ibid.

4. Joseph Campbell with Bill Moyers, *The Power of Myth* (New York: Doubleday, 1988), p. 72.

Chapter 6. How Anansi Got God's Stories

1. Harold Courlander, *A Treasury of African Folklore: The Oral Literature, Traditions, Myths, Legends, Epics, Tales, Recollections, Wisdom, Sayings, and Humor of Africa* (New York: Marlowe & Company, 1996), p. 188.

2. Clyde W. Ford, *The Hero With an African Face: Mythic Wisdom of Traditional Africa* (New York: Bantam Books, 1999), p. 158.

3. D. M. Dooling, "The Wisdom of the Contrary: A Conversation With Joseph Epes Brown," *Parabola*, vol. IV, no. 1, p. 62.

4. Joseph Campbell, *The Masks of God: Primitive Mythology* (New York: Penguin Books, 1977), pp. 273–274.

5. Scott Leonard, "Trickster Myths: The Embodiment of Ambiguities," *Myth in Literature*, n.d. <http://cc.ysu.edu/~saleonar/trickster_myths.htm> (July 12, 2002).

Chapter 7. Kwasi Benefo in the Land of the Dead

1. Camilla L. Greene, "Myth Connections." *Yale-New Haven Teachers Institute*, 2001 <http://www.yale.edu/ynhti/curriculum/units/1983/2/83.02.08.x.html> (July 15, 2002).

2. Harold Courlander, *A Treasury of African Folklore: The Oral Literature, Traditions, Myths, Legends, Epics, Tales, Recollections, Wisdom, Sayings, and Humor of Africa* (New York: Marlowe & Company, 1996), pp. 94–95.

FURTHER READING

Abdulai, David. *Sankofa: Stories, Proverbs, and Poems of an African Childhood*. Denver, CO: Dawn of a New Day Publications, 1995.

Abrahams, Roger D. *African Folktales*. New York: Pantheon Books, 1983.

Ardagh, Philip. *African Myths and Legends*. Parsippany, NJ: Dillon Press, 1999.

Frobenius, Leo. *African Genesis: Folk Tales and Myths of Africa*. Mineola, NY: Dover Publications, 1999.

Gale, Steven H., compiler. *West African Folktales*. Lincolnwood, IL: NTC Publishing Group, 1995.

Goss, Linda, ed. *Jump Up and Say! A Collection of Black Storytelling*. New York: Simon & Schuster, 1995.

Smith, Alexander McCall. *Children of Wax: African Folk Tales*. New York: Interlink Publishing Group, 1999.

Tembo, Mwizenge. *Legends of Africa*. New York: MetroBooks, 1998.

INTERNET ADDRESSES

African Folk Tales

Retellings of several South African myths for teachers and students.

<http://www.canteach.ca/elementary/africa.html>

African Stories Treasure Trove: Online Animal Stories From Africa

Retellings from many African tribes, from the Kennedy Center "African Odyssey" project.

<http://artsedge.kennedy-center.org/aoi/literary/ storytelling/trove.html>

Tales, Fables, and Stories From Africa

Online retellings of some lesser-known stories.

<http://quattro.me.uiuc.edu/~fog/tales.html>

✺ INDEX ✺

transformation myth, 66–67, 68, 70, 72, 75
trickster, 78, 79, 80–82, 84, 88–89
tropical forest, 8

U

underworld, 92, 96, 97, 98, 99, 102
United States, 88

Y

Yataa, 56, 58, 60
Yoruba, 18–19, 28, 78

Z

Zambezi River, 41
Zeus, 51
Zimbabwe, 13